5.95

D0992754

CHINESE

PAPER-CUT

PICTURES

OLD AND MODERN

Frontispiece:
HOPEI (Wei district).   *top: Cow resting; centre: cock pecking;*
bottom: Chi-lin playing with the sun, mythical animal

NANCY KUO

photographs by GUY DAVIS

CHINESE PAPER-CUT PICTURES

OLD AND MODERN

LONDON / ALEC TIRANTI / 1964

PRINTED BY HOLMESDALE PRESS LTD., REDHILL
BOUND BY MANSELL LTD., LONDON N.1.

© 1964 ALEC TIRANTI LTD., 72 CHARLOTTE STREET, LONDON W.1.

MADE AND PRINTED IN THE UNITED KINGDOM

ACKNOWLEDGEMENTS

My love of Chinese paper-cut was stimulated by the first publication on this subject, *Window Flowers* by Chen Su-liang, published in China in 1947, which I discovered by accident in a small Chinese bookshop in Rangoon. Not until 1963, when the secretary of the Britain-China Friendship Association asked me whether I could help to organise some exhibitions of the Chinese paper-cuts which had arrived in London from Peking, did I fully realize the significance of this folk art.

Since then the Horniman Museum has acquired a set of the exhibits, and the touring exhibition has met with appreciation at various museums and art colleges throughout the country. Up to now thirteen exhibitions have been arranged, and there have been three television presentations. My own lectures have perhaps also helped towards an understanding of this simple yet complex art.

The present book has been published to satisfy my audiences, and also to present these fine examples of this unique art, to a wider public.

I am greatly indebted to friends, especially Miss Chen Yao-hua and Mr. Wu Hung-nien, who have helped me in collecting some very valuable paper-cuts for my illustrations, and also to the Chinese People's Association for Cultural Relations with Foreign Countries, for their generous assistance in the provision of many books. Without these, my own book would not have been possible.

CONTENTS

INTRODUCTION

Never before has China been so conscious of her cultural heritage. Great efforts are being made to preserve and develop her traditional arts and crafts; yet at the same time she is speeding towards modernisation and industrialisation.

It is indeed a phenomenon that an equilibrium can be obtained when two such contrasting movements are present. Young in spirit, mature in time, China has adopted or assimilated all that is good for her within or beyond her borders and stamped it with her genius.

The investigation into paper-cuts is one of the numerous activities of the present-day efforts to preserve her traditional arts. It is a rich gold mine. The achievements by the peasant of the past with little or no education, have shown wisdom and artistic talents, even though they were limited by the use of very simple tools and materials.

Paper-cut is the cheapest form of decoration. It was used to decorate a large building, or something as small as a cake. But to treat it as purely decorative, is to diminish its greatness. The best of the monochrome paper-cuts, some near-abstract images of animals or men, have such vitality and beauty that they are indeed an outstanding art form.

There are certain affinities between Chinese painting and paper-cut. First of all their basic material is paper; both are lineal; both are noted for their rich vocabulary and their abbreviated phrases; at times the picture content of both is metaphorically made up of signs and symbols.

Yet with all this close affinity, Chinese painting and paper-cut are distinctly far apart from each other. Although there were more men than women among the painters, and more women than men among the creators of paper-cut, the latter is an art more vigorous, direct and intense and primitive. While painting excels in its subtleness and grace, the paper-cut bursts with the joy of life.

This optimism in folk art has persisted through the ups and downs of many centuries. Optimism ascends still higher, and the will to live and create is shown in the latest works classified as New Creations.

The paper-cuts are as flat as the Chinese paintings—three dimensions are not required. The ingenuous peasant had innovated a kind of composition, contrast and graduation of tones, and characterisation of people which is very typical of the paper-cuts. The use of positive and negative patterns, or the contrasting positive and negative outlines of a picture, is fully explored with many successful results.

It is said that the shadow play cut-out influenced the art of paper-cut, or vice versa. This is possible. Perhaps we should put it this way: the paper-cut was practised long before shadow play was initiated; and after the peasants had mastered paper-cutting, they began to use their craft in cutting out theatrical figures in stronger materials: skins of sheep, donkeys or oxen. And when both arts were flourishing the influence could have been a two-way traffic.

Chinese paper-cuts are produced in almost every region. The best are from the North West provinces (Shensi, Kansu, Ningsia—now Inner Mongolia), Shansi, Hopei, Shantung, Chekiang, Kiangsu and Kwangtung provinces. The illustrations in this book are selected from these provinces, and although small in number, they clearly show the diversity of styles, mediums and techniques.

HISTORICAL BACKGROUND

The Chinese, inventors of paper, used that material profusely in life and in the arts. Many of us are aware that Chinese water colour painting is one of the great achievements of the world, but few know of paper-cuts. After twenty years of investigation, this art has emerged as one possessing a quality and scope, unique in its field.

The first book on the subject, as stated above, was *Window Flowers*, 1947. Since then some forty books on the art have appeared in China and a few abroad. Yet research is still going on, especially on the historical background and the origins of paper-cuts. The latest book, *Paper-cut Research*, published in 1962, provides further information on this aspect, but we are only at the beginning. The author of this latter book, Cheng Chih-yu, quotes writings from different sources mainly of T'ang and Sung Dynasties, indicating that in the T'ang period, paper-cut decorations were used by men in the street and the noble alike; that if a woman learned the skill of embroidery and paper-cutting before she married, she would gain the respect of her husband's family and the love of her husband.

It is said that the Spring Festival is the greatest occasion for the display of this art, and of other folk arts. Emperors of the T'ang Dynasty used to entertain their courts at the beginning of the Spring Festival, and at the arrival of his courtiers, each was given a colourful silk flag decorated with gold and silver cut-outs in the form of lettering and flowers. Sometimes the emperor might request the scholar officers to write improvised poetry when a paper-cut Spring Flower was bestowed on them. In the household of the nobles, small Spring Flags were cut out from gold and silver or coloured papers, and were used as decorations to tie under the flower bushes or to pin to ladies' hair.

Paper-cuts in the form of butterflies or sparrows were also used for hair decoration. Whether the men shared their womenfolk's fashion or not is not mentioned, but it has been written that during one of these gay festivals, Su Tung-Po, a great poet of the Sung Dynasty, was seen walking with little Spring Flags pinned to his hair—much to the amusement of the younger members of his family.

Judging by the fact that women were encouraged to learn both the art of embroidery and paper-cut, we can assume that paper-cuts were used for embroidery patterns, and as paper was invented in the Han Dynasty when the standard of embroidery was very high, it is logical to assume that the art of paper-cutting was initiated at that time.

THE CREATORS

No creator's name was attached to any of the paper-cuts until recently, and all the old traditional motifs are therefore anonymous. They are works perfected by the collective efforts of countless individuals who contributed and blended their imagination and skill for centuries.

Like other folk arts in many countries, some of the paper-cut patterns were carried on from generation to generation within a family, eventually spreading to the whole of their region or to other provinces.

Of all the creators, the peasant women form the largest group. Young girls of the Chekiang, Shantung and Kirim regions have to learn the art of paper-cutting, embroidery, sewing and cooking before marriage. During the wedding, the intelligence and character of the bride is judged by the amount of work she has done, and the standard of her embroidery and paper-cuts.

There are some peasant families who do paper-cutting as a subsidiary line, and sell paper-cuts in the markets during the New Year. They are the semi-professional people, and the working unit is the family. The leader of the team who does the cutting may be the wife or the husband, the children or relatives of the family will help to dye the paper, sharpen the knives or scissors, or any other work. Sometimes in some families, the distribution is more systematic, each member might be made an expert in a particular job.

The smallest group consists of the professional craftsmen who devote all their life to paper-cutting, and roam the cities selling their work. For them, the New Year is the great selling day, when every family is renewing the decoration in the house, preparing gift parcels, and women look for new embroidery patterns in the paper-cuts of the day. This does not mean that these professionals do not do business at other times; embroidery patterns are sold at all times of the year, and paper-cuts are used for funerals as well as festive occasions including weddings and birthdays. Yet in the past, these highly skilled craftsmen led a very difficult life; they had no status even though their art was popular.

During the past fourteen years, appreciation has come from art circles with the backing of the government. The craftsmen's work and living are being taken care of, the best of the craftsmen being invited to teach in the craft centres or art academies. Artists, too, have joined in, producing paper-cuts with new themes; the New Creation is the result of a combined effort of craftsmen and artists.

Collections of paper-cuts are now going on, many books dealing with regional selections have been published, exhibitions and competitions of paper-cuts are being arranged by various art institutes and supported by the government. All this has culminated in a climate of great enthusiasm for this art.

THEMES, SYMBOLISM AND USAGES

The themes used in paper-cut are as varied as those in painting. The peasant artist manipulates his scissors, knife or tool with as much ease as the painter his brush. And like the Chinese painter, he will cut out directly—landscapes, people, animals, flowers, birds and insects including some geometrical patterns—without a preliminary sketch.

Some designs have symbolic meanings. A mythical animal *Chi-lin* (*frontispiece*) will bring babies; the lotus (52), pomegranate and pig (63) also symbolise fertility; peach, pine and crane (40) symbolise longevity; *Yüan-yang* (duck and drake) (56) symbolise fidelity in marriage; bamboos, pine, plum blossom and chrysanthemums (48, 49) represent the unbending spirit of man; dragons (14) lions and tigers (15) are symbols of courage and strength.

Other designs have phonetic allusions; the way to decipher the meaning of the paper-cut in this category is to read the names of their subjects with the phonetic allusion of another word. For example a design with fishes symbolises 'excess of wealth' because, in Chinese, fish and excess are both read as *Yü*; a design with magpie and plum blossoms symbolises 'happiness expressed through one's eyebrows' as magpie and happiness in Chinese both read *si*, and plum blossoms and eyebrows in Chinese both read *mei*; a design composed of a bat and peaches (52) symbolises 'luck and longevity can be obtained together'.

At times Chinese lettering is incorporated into the design to express the people's cherished hopes more openly. Words often used in the past were 'luck', 'longevity', 'happiness', and similar. Nowadays expressions are used, instead of single words, such as 'great leap forward', etc.

The size of paper-cuts varies greatly, from a tiny one-inch cake decoration, to a very large ceiling decoration amounting to several square feet. Large scale designs are cut out in sections, and when completed are pasted together in the required position.

Most of the paper-cuts are independent pictures, but some must be grouped together to form a whole design. For example 'Eight deities going across the sea' consists of a set of eight figure paper-cuts. A set of narrative paper-cuts is composed of numerous separate parts, each depicting a dramatic situation relating to the whole opera. The passionate love of the theatre is clearly shown in the works of many regions, especially in the Hopei and Kwantung provinces.

Paper-cuts are used for interior and exterior decoration. Those pasted to window panes are called Window Flowers; ceilings Ceiling Flowers; door lintels Luck Hangings; others are pasted to columns and walls. These building decorations may remain in place for a year and will be renewed just before the Spring Festival begins.

Paper-cuts called Happy Flowers are pasted on corners of mirrors, paper lanterns, candles, fans, screens, gift packages and offerings: these may have a shorter span of life than those mentioned above.

As for Flower Patterns paper-cuts, they are stuck onto materials intended for embroidery. Here they are transformed into dazzling hues as the embroidress works these patterns on hats, aprons, pillow cases, sleeves, cushions, table cloths, eiderdown covers, tobacco bags, slippers and shoes.

A hundred years ago, paper-cuts were used as sketch patterns for carving connected with buildings, also as stencils for decorating lacquer wares and pottery.

It is said that during the beginning of the Yuen Dynasty, the people in the Su Chow region believed that a paper-cut female figure holding a broom in her hand could help to reduce rainfall. If the rainfall was excessive, the women of the time would cut out the female figure with her broom and hang it under the eaves to pray for a dry day. They believed this paper figure would use her broom to sweep away the rain and thus clear the sky.

In Malaya there are superstitious women who will cut out the form of their husband's mistress and put a needle in its heart or head, hoping fervently that their rival will fall ill and die.

REGIONAL CHARACTER

Generally speaking, central China is the fertile soil for Flower Pattern paper-cuts; in the south Happy Flower paper-cuts prevail; and in the north Window Flower paper-cuts find their best settings.

The art of embroidery is practised in every region and although Kwangtung Province enjoys a reputation few other provinces can rival, Kiangsu Province in central China is, from ancient times, the centre of embroidery work, and here the best silks are produced. The magnificent Nanking brocade, the exquisite Soochow woven silk, the enchanting Changsu embroidered sleeve-bands, all come from this region. It is no wonder that the most beautiful Flower Pattern paper-cuts also come from this area.

Chang Yung-sho who had created ten thousand designs of Flower Patterns is a legend of our time. Born in an artistic but humble family, he began paper-cutting when twelve years old. Like many other peasant artists, he was starving most of the time; hunger and humiliation may have saddened his heart, but it did not dampen his zeal to learn about nature and to create with what he had learned. And what fantastic shapes he created of the chrysanthemums (48, 49).

The Nanking Happy Flower paper-cuts are pictures composed in frames of fruits (gourds, peaches, pears, etc.) or in the shape of diamonds, squares, rectangles or ovals. They are renowned for their boldness and excellent compositions. A cock cut-out with a few broad lines radiates with vitality and sparkle (42). The lyrical cutting of a little cowherd playing a flute whilst on the back of his buffalo (41) was conveyed by a few lines and broad planes. The wild forest scene where deer and crane are playing among bamboo groves and pine trees (40) is at once serene and yet full of rhythmic movement—these near-abstract and symbolic pictures are joys to behold.

Next to this region and sharing a similar rich cultural background is Chekiang Province. Hanchow city was described by men of letters as the most beautiful place in the world. It is also known for its fine silk. Another famous city in the southern part of Chekiang is Wenchow, an art centre known for its cross-stitch embroideries, umbrellas, abacuses, mats, boxwood carvings and inlaid wood articles. The paper-cut from this city is noted for fine craftsmanship. The fishes and squirrels (47) pattern composed in octagonal form, is an example of the most intricate tracery work on paper known to man. The skill required to undertake such work is supreme.

In Hopei province one encounters the dazzling Window Flower of rainbow hues. The most outstanding character of the work of this province is the traditional theatrical figures carved out from thin white (*Hsuen*) papers coloured with dyes. Of these, Wei district (44-46) is famous all over the country. The craftsmen living in this fertile plain surrounded by mountains are highly skilled and may rightly claim to be the leading masters in knife craft.

The most celebrated artist amongst them was Wang Lao-shan, a peasant who was madly in love with Peking Opera. He was a man of great sensibility, keen observation and lively mind. Nothing was too much trouble in his probing into the mystery of life and of art. He believed that art is a communication and the artist is not only the giver but also the receiver. He believed that the interchange of ideas between the artists and between the artists and their customers is the only way to exalt and enrich art. Born in 1890, he started colouring Window Flowers at the age of seven, and at twelve he gained proficiency in cutting intricate patterns. He soon created new designs of his own which were copied by craftsmen all over the Hopei region *(end papers)*.

It is said that he had produced over two hundred groups of theatrical characters and two hundred groups of flowers and birds patterns within fifty years, yet never neglected his farm work.

Among his favourite characters in his figure work are the good and brave ones, which he drew from folklore, novels or Peking Opera. He produced numerous paper-cuts of the witty and powerful Monkey King from the *Western Journey*, the tender and brave Lady White Snake from the *Romance of the White Snake*, the militant heroine Mu Kwei Ying and many other well-known characters, with great understanding and dynamic postures.

Of all the paper-cuts, I consider the cruder and bolder types from Shansi and North West Provinces the most representative, and of immense strength. The simple paper-cuts of fisherman (1), monkey smoking (3), family travelling in horse-cart (5), woman spinning (17), heroine Mu Kwei Ying (20), flying bird (10), cock (11), flower cat (8), Pekinese (7), and many other images of humans and animals, were created with great power of imagination. These are masterpieces, at once abstract and real, vital and beautiful. They are quite different in stylisation compared with Chinese painting, and represent the best aspect and the effectiveness of paper-cutting.

The traditional paper-cuts of this region have strongly influenced the woodcut artists for some twenty years and is now influencing the cutters of the New Creation group.

The salient features of the work of this group of artists are the images of young and enthusiastic children. They are happy, busy bees engaging in a chain of activities, and all seem to be enjoying their work as much as playing. These motifs are to be found in the midst of flying kites, flute playing, fly catching, dragon dance, drum dance, lantern dance, watering of plants, eliminating insects from the grape vine, galloping to school on horseback with the resolution of 'make progress every day', and a little girl picking up a broom to sweep the floor while mother is nursing baby and sewing at the same time. These are some of the motifs of this new group, a purposeful, self-reliant and busy community.

The comparatively dry climate of this region enables people to use a kind of tough but translucent paper, called *Kao-li* paper, to paste onto each small pane of the window. The art of window decoration began here, and the name Window Flowers evolved from it. Perhaps the Shadow Play invented during the Sung Dynasty was inspired by these magical window pictures.

Kwangtung Province is a great seaport of China, and it had contacts with the outside world much earlier than other provinces. It was here that the Sun Yet-sen revolution started, and it was here that the new movement in art—the Linghan School was established. It is a commercial, political and art centre of south China. Paper-cuts created in this region are very rich, and their expressions vary from person to person, and from district to district.

Fatshan city is famous for its pottery and paper-modelling (*papier mâché*) as well as for its great variety of decorative paper-cuts. Monochrome paper-cuts for interiors and gift parcels or offerings were mostly with traditional motifs with a certain distinctive flavour. The silver and golden paper-cuts are colour-ful pictures quite different from those of Hopei Province. The outlines of peonies and phoenix, Chi-lin, flower baskets, goldfish and dragon boats, were carved out of copper or tin foils with fine sharp knives. Glossy coloured papers were then cut separately and pasted onto the back of the shining outlines. This technique recalled the ancient Spring Flags of the T'ang Dynasty which were made in a similar way.

The paper bird is a white paper-cut motif painted with a kind of poster colour, and it has a close affinity with modern Western design, yet with its own unmistakably Chinese rhythm and subject matter.

Theatrical characters are often seen among the colour and monochrome paper-cuts; the best are among the latter and their creators can be named.

Chen Pin Hsing (24) and Hsin Chai Shen (25) are very skilled in cutting dramatic scenes expressed in thin electrifying lines. These fine lines seem to be always moving, and the way they expand and contract abruptly adds interest to the composition. In these pictures, the symbols are vibrant and suggestive, full of magical charm and drama. These two creators came from Chao Yang District, and both knew the art of dissecting and recon-structing, and they did it with feeling and wit.

Chiang Ken Ho (22, 23), another woman of great talent in paper-cutting, lives in Chao Chow city. She is known for her continuous narratives connected with numerous well-loved dramas. Like Wang Lo-Shan, she often visited the theatres and can remember by heart all the characters of each opera and she cuts them directly without sketches. Her favourite characters are those brave, beautiful girls who dared to act against their parents' wills, and married men of their own choosing. Ying Ying of the *Romance of the Western Chamber*, the weaver of the *Cowherd and the Weaver*, Wu Nien of the *Chen Shan and Wu Nien* are but a few of the heroines who went through hell and fire for their true loves.

Her style is opposite to that of the previous two artists. The lines are thick and at times the body is a solid mass filled with negative patterns. She is very original in her composition, especially in the treatment of interior scenes. The paper-cut depicting Liang visiting his beloved (22), is most ingenuous. It shows the waiting room smaller in scale than the bigger drawing room where the old gentleman is telling his daughter that Liang is waiting to see her in the other room. These pictures were cut with scissors, a few at a time, and are therefore now very difficult to obtain.

There are a few other names known in Kwangtung region, and that of Yang Hsueh-Yu stands out from the rest because of his bold and decorative style. His cock is the symbol of strength, and his phoenix (26) a symbol of grace. This latter is an imaginative form of the queen of the birds of rare beauty and majesty.

COLOURS

While black prevails in Chinese painting, red has predominated in paper-cuts. Among all the delightful colours of green, powder blue, pink, purple, orange, yellow and brown, red came out the strongest and brightest.

To the Chinese, red is a symbol of grandeur, dignity, royalty, courage, youth and beauty. It excites and stimulates fiery joy, it penetrates into every household from palace to poor man's hut. The words 'crimson countenance' in Chinese classical literature conveys to the Chinese mind an image of a beautiful young woman, while a 'vermilion door' represents a noble household. In the palace, columns and walls were painted red; there were red silk curtains, carved red lacquer thrones, red tassels for the lanterns, red candles were burning, and red robes were often worn. Even in the austere temples, columns were painted red as in the palace, and red silk hangings embroidered with gold threads were placed in front of and around the Buddhas. And in the theatre, the streets and homes of every Chinese family during the New Year festivities, the wedding and all festive occasions, red was used extensively. Red is life, joy and light; daybreak is described as 'red sun rising high'.

TECHNIQUE

Cutting with scissors. The simplest type of paper-cutting is that of cutting a piece of red paper with a pair of scissors. Very sharp, well pointed scissors will work very well. Whether a pattern should be drawn first on the paper or not, depends on the skill of the person. The novice will certainly need to use a ready-made pattern, or draw one up to guide the cutting, while the expert will cut direct, be it an old traditional pattern or a new design.

When cutting symmetrical work, one may fold the paper many times either from the centre—if a round pattern is required, or fan-fold the paper like the folding sliding door—if the pattern is rectangular. These techniques are more suited to repetitive geometrical patterns and are the easiest way to produce designs without preconceived ideas. The cutter may produce new abstract patterns in this way when other ideas are running out.

Cutting and carving alternatively. For more complicated patterns, part can be cut with scissors, and other parts by carving with different size knives, gouges and punches. Sometimes needles are used to produce fine dotted lines for small general details, once the outline has been cut out.

Carving. This method is mostly done by professional craftsmen for mass production. Many sheets of very fine thin paper are cut at one go. The paper used must be thin and unsized, the knives and tools very sharp. When less than twenty layers of paper are carved at one time, it is necessary to tack the design and the sheets together with needle and thread. But if more copies are needed, say fifty to seventy, then the whole stack of paper sheets are placed inside a wood frame with specially prepared substance under the bottom paper to provide a flexible base for carving. This substance is composed of a vegetable oil and resin.

The design on top and the rest of the stack of paper sheets are then fastened down with nails before the cutting starts. In this way very many patterns can be produced at one operation. Motifs composed of small circles, triangles, half-moon shapes, teeth shapes, etc. can be quickly cut by the use of specially made gouges, chisels and punches. The tools for paper-cutting are mostly made by the craftsmen themselves or ordered to be made for them according to their special requirements; therefore they are not commodities generally available to the public with the exception of scissors. It is not possible to buy Chinese paper-cutting tools in England but I have discovered that among the range of 'X-acto' knives (obtainable from most hobby shops) many are very useful for this art. I would suggest getting knives No. 1, No. 16, No. 17; chisel No. 23; punch No. 31; gouges C and E, and a pair of pointed embroidery scissors. More pointed and narrower scissors can be obtained from surgical instrument suppliers, also a pair of curved nail scissors from a good chemist.

The base for cutting the paper can be an old magazine, a wood board or linoleum. When starting to cut or carve through many layers of papers tacked together with thread, start carving the smallest details first, then carve or cut the bigger patterns, and finally cut the outline with scissors.

When the cutting is completed, dyes are applied to the top of the stack and these soak through all the layers until they reach the bottom sheet. To prevent the spread of the colours, alcohol is added to the dyes. When all the colours applied are dry, the paper-cuts are ready to be taken to the market for sale. They are separated at the market one by one in front of the customer. The dyes used might vary from craftsman to craftsman, but the most commonly used are aniline, cinnabar and lazulite dyes. When the paper-cuts are Window Flowers, the designer has to take into consideration that light should pass through, and the colours used must therefore be bright and pure so that a translucent effect results.

Smoked patterns. To do these, first lay a piece of white paper on a wooden board. Then put the paper-cut pattern on top of the white paper and spread water over them. This will hold them together. Lift up the board and turn it upside down above an oil lamp and allow the black smoke of the flame to cover the entire surface of the pattern and paper. When the old paper-cut is dried by the heat it can be removed easily, leaving a clean white pattern on a very interesting black-cloud background. In some districts printings were used as patterns.

BIBLIOGRAPHY

Window flowers by Chan Su-liang, 1947
Peking shadow play by Wang Sun, Peking 1953
Window flowers with dramatic scenes from Chekiang by Chiang Feng, Peking 1954
Nanking paper-cuts by Ho Yen-ming and Chang Tao-i, Shanghai 1956
Chao Chow paper-cuts by Chao Chow Cultural Institute, Peking 1957
Kwantung paper-cuts by Chinese Artists' Union, Kwang Chow branch, Kwang Chow 1957
Kirin paper-cuts by Kirin Province Art Institute for the People, Changchun 1958
Honan paper-cuts by Honan Province Art Institute for the People, Honan 1959
Heilungkiang paper-cuts by Heilungkiang Art Institute for the People, Haerping 1959
Chinese paper-cuts by the People's Fine Art Publishing Society, Peking 1959
Paper-cuts by Wang Tzu-shin, Peking 1960
Pukiang paper-cuts by Chan-yuen, Peking 1960
Chinese paper-cuts by Hejzlar, Czechoslovakia, London 1960
Paper-cut Research by Cheng Chih-yu, Shanghai 1962
Sculpture in paper by Bruce Angrove, London and New York 1957

1. SHANSI. *Fisherman*

2. SHANSI. *Monkey carrying lanterns*

3. SHANSI. *Monkey smoking*

4. SHANSI. *Donkey-cart*

5. NORTH WEST PROVINCES. *Horse-cart*

6. SHENSI. *Camel*

7. SHENSI. *Pekinese*

8. SHENSI. *Flower cat*

9. SHENSI. (*Pheasant*

10. SHENSI. *Flying bird*

11. SHENSI. *Cock*

12. SHENSI. *Cock*

13. SHENSI. *Bird pecking*

14. SHENSI. *Dragon*

15. SHENSI. *Tiger*

16. SHENSI. *Firewood seller*

17. SHENSI. *Woman spinning*

18. SHENSI. *Woman feeding chicken*

19. SHENSI. *Woman gathering mulberry leaves*

20. SHENSI. *Heroine Mu Kwei Ying*

21. SHENSI. Two versions of the beautiful *Tiao Chan*

22. KWANGTUNG (Chao Chow city). *Liang visiting his beloved*, scene from the opera *Liang Shan Pa and Chu Ying Tai* by Chiang Ken Ho

23. KWANGTUNG (Chao Chow city).   *Separation*, scene from the opera
Romance of the Western Chamber by Chiang Ken Ho

Encounter, scene from the opera
24. KWANGTUNG (Chao Chow city).   *A Drop of Water* by Chen Pin Hsing

25. KWANGTUNG (Chao Chow city).

Departure, scene from the opera *Across the River* by Hsin Chai Shen

26. KWANGTUNG (Chao Chow city). *Phoenix*, by Yang Hsueh Yu

27. KWANGTUNG. *Double happiness* pattern

28. **KWANGTUNG** (Fatshan city).   *Dragon head*

29. **KWANGTUNG** (Chao Yang district). *Boys flying kites*, by Hsin Chai Shen

30. SHENSI. *Visiting relatives*

31. *left*: NORTH WEST PROVINCES.   *The warrior*
right: SHENSI.   *Going to a birthday party*

32. SHENSI. *Reconciliation,* by Wang Cheng Chen

33. **SHANSI** *Tiger*

34. HOPEI (Tientsin city). *Sword dance*

35. HOPEI (Tientsin city), *Flying Devas*

36. HOPEI (Tientsin city). *Tien-an-Man*

37. HOPEI (Tientsin city). *The ghost who repels all evils*

38. KWANGTUNG. *Landscape* pattern

39. FUKIEN (Chuan Chow district). Negative pattern

40. KIANGSU (Nanking city). *Crane and deer* pattern

41. **KIANGSU** (Nanking city). *Boy playing flute* pattern

42. KIANGSU (Nanking city). *Cock crow* pattern

43. KWANGTUNG (Fatshan city). *Paper birds*

44. HOPEI (Wei district). *The formidable judge,* theatrical character

45. HOPEI (Wei district). *Hsiang Yü*, theatrical character

46. HOPEI (Wei district). *Learned general*, theatrical character

47. **CHEKIANG.** *Fishes and squirrels* pattern

48. KIANGSU (Yang Chow city). *Chrysanthemum*

49. KIANGSU (Yang Chow city). *Chrysanthemums*

50. KIANGSU. *Flowers and birds*, Flower Pattern for embroidery

51. HOPEI (Wei district). *Romance of Lady White Snake*, theatrical character

52. HOPEI (Wei district)   *left: Fisherman,* theatrical character   *top right: Lotus*
bottom right: Bat and peach

53. KWANGTUNG (Fatshan city). *Phoenix and peonies*

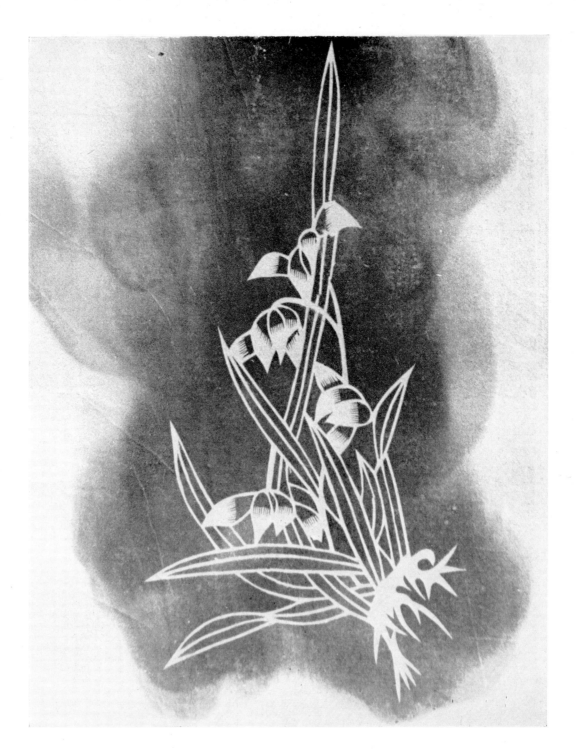

54. Smoked pattern

55. KWANGTUNG (Fatshan city)

left: Embroidery pattern for tobacco bag. *right:* Luck hanging for door lintel

56. KIANGSU (Nanking city). *Yüang-yang* (duck and drake)

57. HONAN. *Ceiling flowers*

58. HOPEI (Peking). *School girl helping in the fields*

59. HOPEI (Peking). *Boy going to school on horseback*

60. HOPEI (Peking). *Boy playing flute*

61. HOPEI (Peking). *Lantern dance*

62. HOPEI (Peking). *Boy watering garden*

63. HOPEI (Peking). *Fertility*

64. HOPEI (Peking). *Woman feeding pig*

65. HOPEI (Peking). *Flower girl, cock and birds*

66. HOPEI (Peking). *Boy offering apple*

67. HOPEI (Peking). *Dragon dance*

68. HOPEI (Peking). *Girls decorating their windows with paper-cuts*

69. HOPEI (Peking). Interior: *Woman sewing*

70. HOPEI (Peking). Interior: *The industrious family*

71. HOPEI (Peking). *The farmer and his wife*

72. HOPEI (Peking).   *Girl on her way to lessons*

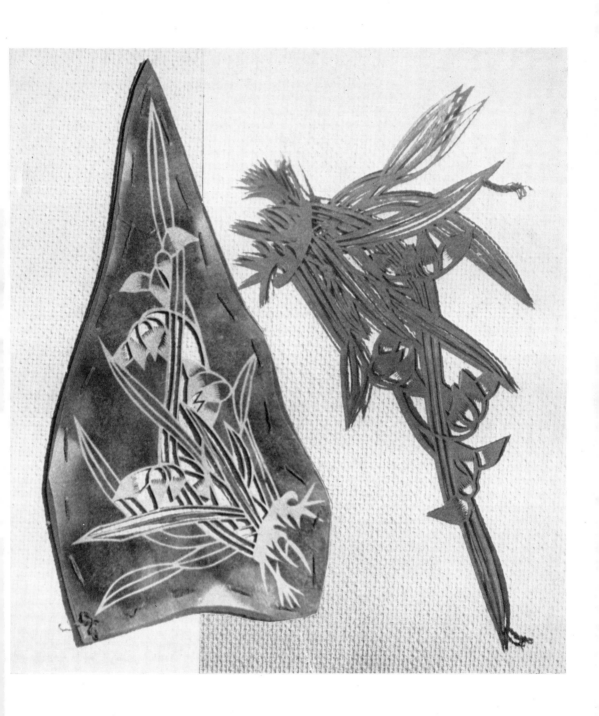

73. A stack of paper sheets tacked together with thread

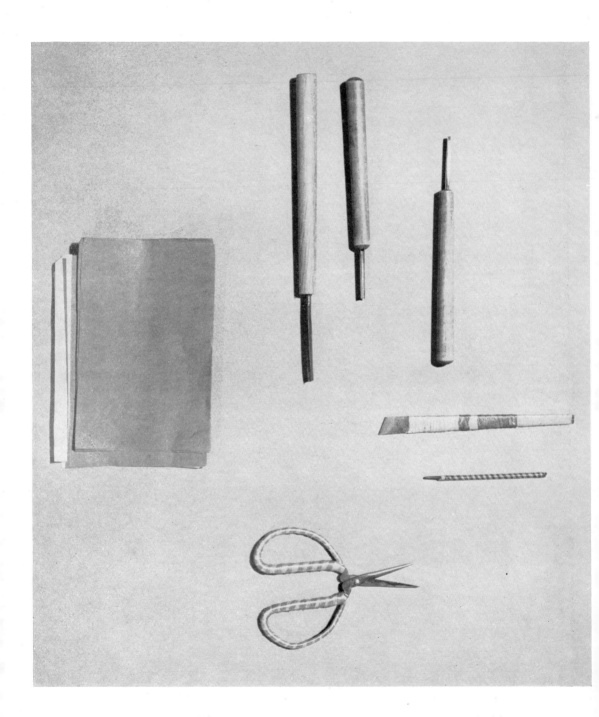

74. Tools: scissors, knife, large and medium gouges, small punch, red and white papers